Taste & See

Neil S. Reddy

RED
FERRET PRESS

Taste & See
Neil S. Reddy

ISBN-10: 0692613722
ISBN-13: 978-0692613726

© 2016 Neil S. Reddy

Published through Red Ferret Press
An extension of Weasel Press
Located in Manvel, TX
http://www.redferretpress.com

Printed in the U.S.A.

Table of Contents

For Dawn

With some inspiration
thanks
 and time
from Lisa.

xx Ned.

An Overture of Heat

Warmth

Beneath palms and limbs

Her body shifts

Gives

Softens

As her pulse quickens,

As muscles agree

With a sigh

With scent

and fluid grace,

They signal their

welcome.

Welcome, welcome,

Come on in.

Taste

Opulent

As I could be,

Hedonistic as a baby,

Cigar but sucking,

>I notice the texture is similar

>To that of your left nipple

>Memories come folding in…

Cold champagne

And warm pubic hair…cocktail,

Searching for a glistening pearl…oysters,

Chocolate smeared over right breast,

Tonguing the left – so it won't feel neglected – all heart,

Biting the back of your leg,

Come here,

Try it this way,

I could kiss that neck for a week,

Back to the left breast,

How did I get here?

We aim to please,

Fuck me, scold me,

Hold me with your hidden third hand

And squeeze…

Time for another cigar I believe.

Texture

He took off his clothes and stood in front of the TV,
"Rather presumptuous…" She commented through a
shadow's smile.
"I am going to make love to you. Love you the way you
Deserved to be loved." He replied.
And he did,
Slowly,
With great passion, consideration and skill,
A sensitive lover, he satisfied his girl.

After,
Ten minutes after,
She said,
"Fuck me. Fuck me hard! And fuck me now."

There's just no pleasing some people.

Heat

Flame trickles

Down my gullet,

blackens my centre

with longing,

crazed, desperate beyond bearing,

I explode,

I know nothing but this

closed eye coming,

that shatters me between your hips,

Hold me, hold me,

I have tasted oblivion,

seen death,

Only your hot limbs

can save me now,

Lock me in your embrace,

my brow to your shoulder,

Hands in your hair,

trembling in the stillness

of this precious

aftermath,

Resigned.

Feel

In absolute bliss
You drink mulled wine
From her lips
Swathed in kisses,
Tracing the curves,
Her body tells you to follow,
She murmurs pleasure,
And thrills the passionate ear,
Like ancient secrets, spoken in shadows to the faithful
followers,
Stop
Listen
Absolute awareness now,
This is the sanctuary
Of herself,
Make your entrance,
Devoutly
With measured steps,
Feeling the privilege
All the way,
Now abandon yourself to her,
To the absolute ecstasy
of her.

At Two

If my eyes could feel
The texture of your body,
I would be satisfied
To watch you sleeping,
To watch and wander
With my feeling eyes,
And not disturb
Or steal your time,
I would touch the delicate places
And you would not stir,
I would feel through these eyes
And be satisfied,
Whilst you slept the night through,
If mere seeing were enough,
All this would be true,
But it's not all about me,
Wake up,
Let's talk about you.

Comfort

We sit with silence on our journey,

The sun white on her arm strays with brave fingers

to warm her breast,

We sit with silence and we sit with smiles,

We are comfortable with silence between us,

We can speak with our eyes,

And that is enough.

After

Riddled with happiness,

Strawberry lazy,

Cocktail content and double measure too,

Strong smooth slow suck,

Draws warm through thick straw,

Tongue the texture,

Swallow the brew,

Feel the clawless paw,

Rub the ripple of sorrow away,

The backbone purrs,

Deep and slow,

The easy murmur in every bone,

The sun slips away,

Maybe after all you can face another day,

In moments like these,

You catch yourself thinking,

This must be somebody else's world,

I shouldn't be here,

But you are…

With the warmth of another close by,

Summer in the sheets,

Armchair sunset glow,

Warm sirocco of the soul,

Moments like these let you know,

Life is sweet.

Happy to be fooled,

Wanting it to be true,

You let it ride,

Like a needle in a vinyl groove,

Content to believe,

As long as she is near,

The moment could stick…

Forever

And your heart cries

Fool me some more

Fool me some more

Fool me some more

Mundane Grace

Held cold over the coals. Captive to vain promises,
Vows to a virgin, broken every night, slipping the knot whilst sleeping,
Morning's conscience comes ringing like a ripple, bleating like a babe,
A thousand whimpering reasons whispered why I should be afraid.
Silent and ground as sugar, I thought bitter and shook inside my cage,
Now abroad and breathing freedom straight from the pump,
Straight from the nipple of love,
Breathing sweat and spitting flame,
Now the heat of heart and thigh I obey,
Grasping the hand of another long into the night,
Tight as a tourniquet,
So the thumping pulse of life,
Rises like steam in my veins,
I whistle through my teeth,
I sing with my winking eye,
And bite the rump of love with affection,
Because I was dead but now,
I am alive.

A Car, the Plant and Two Sisters

Nobody laughs like sisters,

And nobody talks like these two,

And nobody is talking to me,

I am just of the plant in the back of the car,

They laugh every time they say it,

Terrific Triffid - Ha ha ha!

(I think it's the motorway lights that do it.)

The traffic slows, we swap lanes, change down a gear,

We, that is, the car, the two sisters and the plant that's me,

Ha ha ha!

Are travelling down to London from over there,

And I just can't believe the laughter of these two can fit

in here,

I think I could mend the world,

Free the nations, bind up the broken-hearted,

Set the captives free, if...

Who am I kidding? Hee hee hee!

But maybe,

I could expand their laughter beyond these four wheels,

And change the faces of those other drivers,

Shrivelled up from the long sucking on this slow crawl

sour jam,

Ha,

But those Boy Scouts in the beat up van,

Better watch out!

The signs say 50, but they should read – Hungry Women!

Warning! Danger! Look Out! Sisters inside!

Ha ha ha!

Travelling loud, singing to the music,

Singing all the wrong words,

Laughter and babble,

There's so much life inside this car,

So much of that rare contraband,

That can make wrong right, turn troubles to victories,

And even make life in the contraflow seem

Beautiful,

But hey,

What do I know?

I'm just the plant in the back of the car.

Ha ha ha!

One in the Eye

Laughing,

Because it's inside

and needs out, despite it all,

the history, the curse,

the desperate, the cruel,

the worse.

Laughing uncontrollably,

Swearing at the movers and makers,

advisor slave traders,

Tarnished and trite,

would-be god's,

Laughing,

Finding,

that despite everything,

Everything they said,

you can laugh,

from the inside,

from the gut,

from beginning to end,

all you had to do

was start.

And in this

And in this stream of life
In which I swim,
I shall find my stroke,
And in this tongue
I shall talk,
And in this space
I shall move,
And in this time
I shall live,
Like no other
For no other,
Other than myself,
And in this
I shall not be bested.

Scar Sky

Air trail slashes open the sky.
  white scar running from sun
    to infinite blue,
Clouds like stretch marks
  show the effort of the day,
Ripple to the colour of scalded flesh,
Healing over time
  as the day is ending
    and we are all
      a little more marked,
        by another day,
The sun, the sky
Me and you,
We should bare them all proudly,
Let the world see,
  Display like the sky,
    so that others can marvel,
Recognise
That they
  Like you
    Like them
      Have survived.

Orgy of...

Start your late night talking,
Start it right now,
Let it roll,
I'll roll along with you
And fix myself a smoke,
Mend the world with your words,
Dissect destiny and reason,
Folly and hope and everything in-between
I'm listening,
I'm in the right frame of mind,
Ragged as road kill, dead on my feet, beaten flat,
I need the spells your mouth can cast,
Ask me anything and answer it yourself,
Get me coffee drunk and nicotine high,
Talk the moon out of the sky,
Talk until the sun breaks the night,
Talk these tears from my eyes,
Don't let the sound of my crumbling bones,
Break your stride,
Whatever you do,
Ignore me,
Just keep on talking,
I'm listening,

You've got me,

Call up all the words you can muster,

And talk,

Talk on,

I'm listening.

Morning with No toast

Watching the city waking,

Even the streets are stretching

And I wonder...

How come I have to be here before the sun?

I watch night's ship dim to a shadow.

The new day has cast off already loaded with care.

The crew ready the sails,

Breath in deep, pull back the covers,

Pull back the curtains,

Tiny light wink on,

Just lit cigarettes in a sniper's eye,

Embers of life flicker below me,

The world's still smoking

Despite all the warnings

Turning sea-sick and dizzy

After the first draw of the day.

I am the posted lookout,

There to shout

So the bike shed boys can run away

Duty has placed me here

With no respect for comfort,

I would rather be watching your waking,

But this morning I am the world's audience,

Voyeur to the dawn,

Standing in the stalls,

Witness to the wrong dawn, but I confess,

My childhood eyes still watch the clouds

Make animals.

Gestation

I'm sick of shooting up
And withering out
I don't want to impregnate
I want to gestate
Commit and grow myself some hate
I'm tired of this bleeding curse
Sloughing off life
Cramped and crabby
Shedding hope month by month
Just to show
I'm getting nowhere against a ticking clock
I want to gestate hate
I want to keep it inside me
Feed it with my blood
Fashion it into a weapon
Visceral and pumping, spirting flame and acid
Kicking out its war dance with its heels
Against hollow xylophone ribs,
To feel it twisting and squirming beneath my skin
Until it comes to term
Only then shall I bear down
Breathing venom through gritted teeth
As life tears its way from me,

Tear me a new one

Tear me apart

A loveless labour

Birthed.

Knowledge

You told me,

Love could not last,

You told me,

The passion, the glory,

All would pass,

It is nature's way,

Spring leads to

Winter's blast,

It's nature's way,

Nothing lasts,

I have watched love come,

I saw love go,

But I'm thinking,

It wouldn't have been,

If you hadn't said so.

Dominate

I bought yellow roses,

Cut the stems at an angle,

Placed them by the bed,

I set out a bottle of chilled white wine,

Two tall stemmed glasses,

By their side,

Closed the curtains,

Lit the candles,

Undressed, bathed

And laid on the bed,

A single rose on my chest…

I waited, knowing

You would come home,

See the note I left downstairs saying,

UPSTAIRS,

Then you'd walk through the bedroom door,

And I'd speak with firmed intent,

  "Come here, come here and…"

You are a memory now,

Far away,

Not here,

But when I sense the gentle scent of roses,

I could swear you're near.

Departure

I'm dying
and you did not notice,
I sit here, with my paint peeling
and you did not see.
You have not looked
at these walls for a long time,
the pictures are long gone,
nothing but their shadows can be seen,
faint outlines of time spent.
Life shrugs and time sheds dust around me,
Circumstance like cobwebs
are deadly in their binding,
and I
have the strongest urge
to leave.
Although I am here,
I have left
and you did not see me leave.

All the Time

I hurt all the time,

when I am swallowing beer,

driving the car,

laying in a continent sized bed,

knowing nothing but what is gone, the moon blue eyes,

the long neck, nipples, legs, kisses,

The tender finger cracking words…

I know how it sounds

and that's how it is,

from the gloss surface

to the elusive core,

from the gross show,

to the shy centre of the man,

Whatever it is,

Whatever I am,

I hurt,

All the time.

Give Up

Give up if you must,

But give up tomorrow,

If the weight has become too much to bear,

Fall and be crushed,

But wait a while and fall tomorrow.

Tomorrow is willing to accept your surrender,

Your defeat.

It will accept your flag,

Wholeheartedly and complete,

So stand a little longer,

Stand today and observe the world's turning,

Fill your hours with want and yearning,

Or fill the hours with stillness,

Strength hardly stirring,

Laugh at the sorrow if you can,

Sorrow for the laughter as you must,

But stand,

Even if you've had all you can swallow,

Even if you fear the light of the day to follow,

Stand today,

Give up if you must,

But give up tomorrow.

Loads of Laughs

I'm having loads of laughs,
Biting my lip,
Kitchen sitting in chip fat spit,
Since you've been gone,
I've laughed a lot about
wet days and damp socks,
But look what you left me with
a broken heart and a
smoking fridge.
It's been the time of my life
since you've been gone.
Everything's splendid, there's nothing wrong
with listening to the radio clones,
and your rabid voice on the answer phone,
My heart's aching like a locked backbone
but how I love living alone.
Life, life and all the best bits,
I'm cold gristle chewing and too stubborn to quit.
Here comes another 70 hour week,
Utterly empty and constantly bleak,
but I'll do alright in my warehouse shoes
with my paper cuts and my tabloid truths,
but it's getting a bit much, when there's nothing for

lunch

but stale eggs and cigarette butts,

And now there's a crack in my favourite mug,

God I just can't get enough of this life, life

And all the best bits,

Cold gristle chewing and too stubborn to quit.

A Meeting of Men

The need for confession,
   Nothing in particular,
Merely madmen comparing notes,
The Brotherhood of Cigarettes -
We are the sum of lighters, flints
and experience.
A campfire in our palms,
    we have been here before,
       many lives ago,
           enacting our roles,
We are men,
       gather round,
         this is all we have,
          this and stories,
Stories of the hunt,
     Ancient rituals,
Glossed, polished,
 and improved for the hearing.
 We are men,
Sharing, our aloneness,
 with cigarettes and liquid spirits,
  We trust no one
    with our hearts,

but give

   slivers of flesh

      to impress.

At Last

It's a foul hemmed morning,
That promises no better,
There is enough space here
To make a longing,
But I don't,
And although the phone never rings,
And the rain drizzles
Like a whimpering girl,
I have a clear mountain top
Of retrospect,
The sleepy soul
Of a well fed town,
Beneath my belt,
And I can come to no other
Conclusion than
I am mended.
Fixed,
Healed
At least for today,
And that rain
That drizzle
Is
And nothing more.

The Last Poem

It happened in the supermarket,

Right there in public,

She came right out and said it,

           "At our age you've got to take care of yourself."

At our age,

Hear the bells toll,

From here on in,

CLANG!

Ask not, for whom,

For your bodies got it in for you.

Here it comes,

Exercise, squash,

Looking hot, sweaty and ridiculous,

Constantly running uphill,

To beat the cholesterol doughboy sludge,

The secret sabotage,

That's surely building up, out of sight and spite.

I can't! I protest, I'm a poet,

Fool – there is no mercy!

           "You'll be a healthy poet then."

Eat your greens they're too good to be true,

Eat well, be good to yourself,

But what if my American readers hear of my transformation,

From lurid bard to lettuce sucking King,

I will be disgraced, defaced, ruined,

What if the Australians hear?

        They'll stop buying my poems,

        They'll stop buying me beer.

There is no mercy.

Flush the chain, there goes my career,

Time has a vicious trend,

So here it is,

the last poem,

The last poem,

before the high fibre,

skimmed milk, low fat,

living end.

A December Rose

A December rose,

Blooming like a sunrise,

In the ice season,

Reflecting, refracting,

Petals as red as passion,

Frosted as a lover's goodbye,

For all its beauty and promise,

Doomed to die,

So I shall not pick it,

But let it be,

And let the winter,

Do the deed for me.

Neil S. Reddy has been slumped over a typewriter
for so long that he has been recategorized as an
angle-poised lamp and is often assailed by strangers
trying to turn him off. Do not pity him. He is a foul
mouthed man and is well able to defend himself - he
once reduced a giraffe to tears with a lingering sneer.
He should never be approached during the hours
of darkness without a beverage. He is an outspoken
opponent of everything ignorant, ugly, stupid or
overpriced. He lives quietly with his family in the U.K
but only because they keep him heavily sedated in a
cupboard with a lock; that will be forever England...
until it sinks into the sea. He has a beard that is older
than many people and contains more wildlife than
many zoos. He has an irrational fear of soup. He feels
nothing but contempt for hamsters. He is not to be
trusted. He is troubled, testy and weird to the bone.
He also writes stories.

more titles from this author

Tales in Liquid Time
Weasel Press, 2014

Not Kafka
Weasel Press, 2015

14798205R00026

Printed in Great Britain
by Amazon.co.uk, Ltd.,
Marston Gate.